ALL ABOUT THE RODEO

RODEO BULL RIDERS

Lynn Stone

Rourke
Publishing LLC
Vero Beach, Florida 32964

www.rourkepublishing.com

Photo credits:
Front cover © Elemental Imaging, back cover © Olivier Le Queinec, all other photos © Tony Bruguiere except page 5 © Sarah Burns, page 11 © Mike Kemmer, page 17 Dennis Oblander, page 19 © TJ Baird, page 21 © Zane Thompson

Editor: Jeanne Sturm

Cover and page design by Nicola Stratford, Blue Door Publishing

Library of Congress Cataloging-in-Publication Data

Stone, Lynn M.
  Rodeo bull riders / Lynn M. Stone.
      p. cm. -- (All about the rodeo)
  Includes index.
  ISBN 978-1-60472-390-8
  1. Bull riding--Juvenile literature. I. Title.
  GV1834.45.B84S86 2009
  791.8'4--dc22
                          2008018793

Printed in the USA

CG/CG

Rourke Publishing

www.rourkepublishing.com – rourke@rourkepublishing.com
Post Office Box 3328, Vero Beach, FL 32964

Table Of Contents

Bull Riding   4

Running the Event   13

The Riders   20

The Bulls   22

The History of Bull Riding   26

Glossary   30

Index   32

Bull Riding

A bull is the biggest, baddest animal in the rodeo. It is a heavyweight with horns, mystique, and **menace** wrapped in muscle. Its eyes can cast a glance that would back down a grizzly. And that's just for starters. Along with brawn, a bull has attitude that can more or less be summed up as, "Stay way out of my way, dude."

Rodeo cowboys have attitude, too. They do not make careers out of backing down from anything, including bulls weighing in at 2,000 pounds (909 kilograms). For bull riders, the jarring ride aboard a bull is just another challenge.

This kicking bull loses its rider as it jolts back to the arena floor.

Bull riding pits one athlete against another.

For many fans, bull riding is the pinnacle of rodeo sport. It pits the will and reflexes of a finely tuned human athlete against the violent twists, kicks, and leaps of a bull. The promise of seeing someone risk life and limb on the back of a humongous, ill-tempered bull draws throngs of spectators.

Watching someone else attempt to ride a very large animal that does not want to be ridden has the makings for great drama.

Bull riding, though, has an additional element: extreme danger. A bucking horse prefers not to be ridden, too, but it neither weighs a ton nor has horns.

More important, a **bronco** does not normally attempt to attack a fallen rider. A bull often does, which is why rodeo **bullfighters** immediately risk their own hides to distract the bucking bull away from a fallen rider. Bullfighters can usually hustle over the fence or into a padded barrel and retreat safely. The bull may butt the barrel and send it rolling like a tire, but the bullfighter inside is well protected.

A rodeo bullfighter keeps a keen eye on the action.

Bullfighters are remarkably brave and effective, but they cannot always save a thrown rider from the horns or hooves of a bull. Bulls often leap with all four feet off the ground, and they are not very careful about where they land.

Human **fatalities** are rare, but they are certainly part of this sport. A bull killed twenty-six year old Lane Frost in 1989 after he had been thrown. (Frost was the subject of a 1994 motion picture, *Eight Seconds*.) Bulls also killed Brent Thurman in 1994 and Canadian Glen Keeley in 2000. Bulls killed at least three more riders in 2007.

A bull hurtles dangerously close to the fallen cowboy.

Extreme danger rides with every out; this rider narrowly escaped being gored.

Still, except in a very few instances, the bucking bull and his rider live to duel on another day. A bull, for example, has an injury that can end his rodeo career only once in nearly 10,000 **outs**, according to the Professional Bull Riders (**PBR**) organization's figures for its events.

Bull riders are athletes in peak condition, and they generally avoid being **gored** or stomped. Researchers, however, are just beginning to gather **data** about the exact number of deaths and serious injuries that bull riders suffer. They hope their research will lead to better protective equipment.

Despite the danger, most rides end with neither injury to rider nor bull.

A rodeo bull often attempts to butt, stomp, or gore anyone nearby.

A high-flying bull is likely to
be a high-scoring bull.

Running the Event

Bull riding is a **roughstock**, or judged event. A ride, or out, is judged only if the rider stays aboard for eight seconds. After eight seconds, the ride is officially over, whether the rider has just been thrown to the dirt or remains on the bull. A longer ride does not earn bonus points for a rider.

Both rider and bull are judged, usually by two judges. Each judge awards a total of 50 points, up to 25 for the bull and 25 for the rider. The record PBR score for a rider is 96.5 points.

A rodeo bullfighter prepares to distract a bull as the rider falls off.

The most explosive bulls are the most difficult to ride. They are also the bulls that earn the most style points, so a competitive rider wants to match his skill against the best bull. A bull earns points for its style whether it bucks for two seconds or the full eight.

High kicks earn style points for the bull.

A rider and bull begin their event in a **chute**, which is tight enough to keep a bull in place and unable to buck. The bull wears a **flank strap**, a soft rope, around its middle. The strap is nothing more than an annoyance.

A 15-year old girl at a rodeo workshop climbs aboard a bull in the chute.

★ An annoyed bull w
★ hind legs outward
    effort to ditch the
★ bull that does not
★ worth anything in

Meanwhile, the rider climbs onto the bull and grasps the bull rope in a gloved hand. The rope is wrapped around the bull directly behind its front legs. It is by no means a steering wheel. It is, however, the only place where the cowboy can get a good grip. His spurs will give him some grip and balance, but the bull rope is his lifeline.

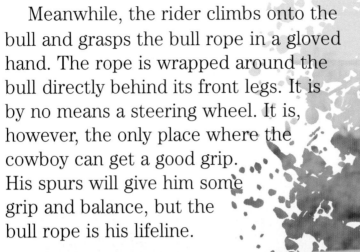

purs are small, pointed, steel wheels fixed to a frame tached to the cowboy's boots. Spurs have dull points, they neither cut nor scratch the bull.

Riders in the PBR wear protective vests. Growing numbers of bull riders, in PBR competition and elsewhere, wear helmets and protective masks, although they are not required. Eventually protective equipment may be as common as cowboy hats and boots.

This acrobat of a bull will not give the cowboy eight seconds up.

When the bull is released, time for the run starts. If the rider lasts eight seconds, he has completed the ride and it is judged. Many rides are never finished, especially aboard the most explosive bulls. The 2007 champion bull, weighing 1,960 pounds (891 kilograms), had the unlikely name *Chicken on a Chain*. Don't be fooled by the name: Chicken on a Chain allowed the average rider to stay aboard for just 3.5 seconds!

It is no disgrace to be thrown before reaching the 8-second standard. The 2007 PBR champion rider, Justin McBride, attempted 89 bulls and rode 57 of them for eight seconds. Even champions get dumped early!

A rodeo bullfighter leaps to take a thrashing bull's attention away from a fallen rider.

The Riders

Bull riders often begin their careers when they are kids, especially if they grow up in a traditional ranch or rodeo environment. Some of them begin riding animals when they are preteens. Professional bull rider J.B. Mauney began riding sheep when he was three.

Bull riding is dominated by men. DeeDee Crawford, however, is a multi-talented cowgirl. She holds the 2007 women's bull riding title and also excels in bronc riding.

Some bull riders are living legends. Larry Mahan was not only a champion bull rider twice, but also rodeo's all-around champion seven times. "Tuff" Hederman was a champion rider who is today the president of Championship Bull Riding (CBR), a professional organization. Justin McBride is a current bull riding star, having won two of the last three PBR world titles. In 2007 he earned $1.8 million in prize money.

Chip off the old block, a youngster rides a calf to the cheers of his bull riding father.

The Bulls

Do not confuse rodeo bull riding with the bullfights of Spain and Mexico. Those fights end with the death of the bull in the arena. Rodeo bulls are valuable properties, and they are treated with care. A champion bucking bull can be worth $100,000 or more.

After its one brief appearance in the rodeo, this prize bull will be retired for the day.

A bull generally reaches its **prime** when it weighs between 1,700 and 1,800 pounds (771 to 816 kilograms), and reaches five or six years of age. Each bull is ridden just once a day. Because they are treated with care, the best performing bulls can remain on the rodeo circuit for several seasons.

A bull chases a bullfighter before leaving the arena. After many rides over time, bulls seem to know when eight seconds have passed and they leave arenas quite easily.

Big bulls can be just as acrobatic as smaller bulls.

The largest bulls weigh up to 2,200 pounds (998 kilograms). Smaller bulls are used in junior and women's events.

✧ **Livestock contractors** provide rodeos with bulls. They usually buy or lease the animals from ranches that specialize in raising bulls that are likely to be athletic and energetic in the rodeo.

The distinct Brahman **breed** with its tall hump has been associated with rodeo bulls for many years. Most bucking bulls today are a mix of breeds, although many still have a portion of Brahman.

Brahma bulls have been part of rodeo bull genetics for a long time.

The History of Bull Riding

Unlike many rodeo sports, bull riding was not one of the necessary ranch and range skills of western cowboys. There was nothing useful to be gained by riding a bull. But after bronc riding was established, bull riding became the next great challenge.

The arena floor remains dangerous immediately after a cowboy is thrown from a bull.

Bull riding first appeared in rodeos as an exhibition rather than a competitive sport, probably in the 1920s. But by the end of the 1920s, bull riding was beginning to gain an enthusiastic audience and sport status.

Bull riding has become so popular in recent years that a small group of bull riders formed their own organization, the Professional Bull Riders (PBR), in 1993 and took their bull riding rodeo show on the road.

Bull riding champion B. J. Schumacher competes aboard Gunner in the National Finals Rodeo.

Meanwhile, the Professional Rodeo Cowboys Association (PRCA) continues to sponsor its bull riding events at PRCA rodeos throughout the country. In addition, bull riding is part of the program at other pro events and many **amateur** events nationwide. A small number of women participate in bull riding at Women's Professional Rodeo Association (WPRA) events.

Fans love the bullfighters who lure bulls away from downed riders.

The popularity of bull riding is at an all time high as professional events are broadcast nationally on television.. Bull riding most likely will please even more fans in the future. However, look for greater attention to bull riders' safety in the near future. The goal is to make the bull rider's wild ride a safer ride.

Glossary

amateur (AM-uh-chur): one who competes for something other than money

breed (BREED): a particular kind of domestic animal within a larger, closely related group, such as the Brahman within the cattle group

bronco (BRON-ko): a bucking horse

bullfighters (BUL-fite-urz): rodeo cowboys who distract bucking bulls after a bull rider has been thrown

chute (SHOOT): a tight, high-sided space in which individual animals can be contained and kept apart from each other

data (DAY-tuh): information gathered by a careful, practiced method

fatalities (fay-TAL-uh-teez): deaths

flank strap (FLANGK STRAP): a band tied around a bull's flanks to encourage bucking behavior

gored (GORD): to have been wounded by a sharp object, especially by an animal's horn

livestock contractors (LIVE-stok KON-trakt-urz): those who raise, and sell or lease, horses or cattle for rodeo use

menace (MEN-iss): that which promises or suggests danger

prime (PRIME): the time of peak condition for competition

outs (OUTZ): the number of times an animal is actually released to be ridden

PBR (PBR): Professional Bull Riders, an organization of bull riders that sponsors its own bull riding events nationwide

roughstock (RUHF-stok): referring to rodeo's judged events with broncos and bulls

Further Reading

Want to learn more about rodeos? The following books and websites are a great place to start!

Books

Halvorson, Marilyn. *Bull Riders*. Orca, 2003.

Kubke, Jane and Jessica Kubke. *Bull Riding*. Rosen, 2006.

Liny, Stephen. *Professional Bull Riding Fan Guide*. Sports Publishing, 2008.

Websites

http://www.pbrnow.com
http://prorodeo.org
www.nlbra.com

Index

bull rope   16
bullfighters   7, 8
bullfights   22
Brahman breed   25
Championship Bull Riding   20
Crawford, Dee Dee   20
fatalities   8
flank strap   15
Hederman, "Tuff"   20
helmets   17
judges   13
masks   17
Mahan, Larry   20
Mauney, J.B.   20

McBride, Justin   19, 20
outs   10
points   13, 14
Professional Bull
   Riders (PBR)   10, 17, 27
Professional Rodeo Cowboys
   Association   28
spurs   16
Women's Professional Rodeo
   Association   28

About The Author

Lynn M. Stone is a widely published wildlife and domestic animal photographer and the author of more than 500 children's books. His book *Box Turtles* was chosen as Outstanding Science Trade Book and Selectors' Choice for 2008 by the Science Committee of the National Science Teachers' Association and the Children's Book Council.